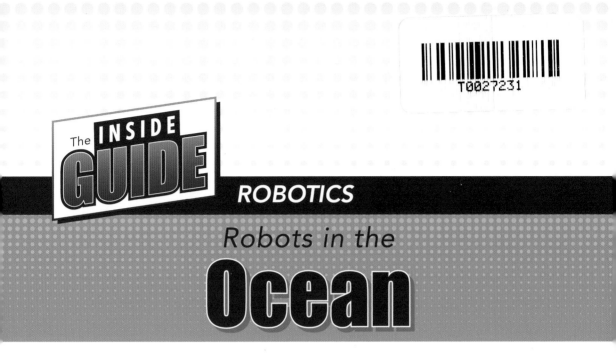

The INSIDE GUIDE

ROBOTICS

Robots in the

Ocean

By Menna Landon

Cavendish Square

New York

Published in 2022 by Cavendish Square Publishing, LLC
243 5th Avenue, Suite 136, New York, NY 10016

Portions of this work were originally authored by Daniel R. Faust and published as *Underwater Robots (Robots and Robotics)*. All new material this edition authored by Menna Landon.

All websites were available and accurate when this book was sent to press.

Library of Congress Cataloging-in-Publication Data

Names: Landon, Menna, author.
Title: Robots in the ocean / Menna Landon.
Description: New York : Cavendish Square Publishing, [2022] | Series: The inside guide: robotics | Includes index.
Identifiers: LCCN 2020043695 | ISBN 9781502660725 (library binding) | ISBN 9781502660701 (paperback) | ISBN 9781502660718 (set) | ISBN 9781502660732 (ebook)
Subjects: LCSH: Oceanography–Juvenile literature. | Robots–Juvenile literature.
Classification: LCC GC11.2 .L36 2022 | DDC 623.82/7–dc23
LC record available at https://lccn.loc.gov/2020043695

Editor: Caitie McAneney
Copyeditor: Jill Keppeler
Designer: Deanna Paternostro

The photographs in this book are used by permission and through the courtesy of: Cover BORIS HORVAT/Staff/AFP/Getty Images; pp. 4, 9 (bottom) Graphic_BKK1979/iStock/Getty Images Plus/Getty Images; pp. 5, 6 Mondadori Portfolio/Contributor/Mondadori Portfolio Premium/Getty Images; p. 7 Lev Fedoseyev/Contributor/TASS/Getty Images; p. 8 Handout/Handout/Getty Images News/Getty Images; p. 9 (top) Dorling Kindersley/Getty Images; p. 10 noraismail/Shutterstock.com; pp. 12 (top), 28 (top) Alexis Rosenfeld/Contributor/Getty Images News/Getty Images; pp. 12 (bottom), 16 Bettmann/Contributor/Bettmann/Getty Images; pp. 13, 19 (bottom), 29 (bottom) picture alliance/Contributor/picture alliance/Getty Images; pp. 14, 15 Ralph White/The Image Bank Unreleased/Getty Images; p. 18 AFP/Stringer/AFP/Getty Images; p. 19 (top) Kurita KAKU/Contributor/Gamma-Rapho/Getty Images; p. 20 SAEED KHAN/Contributor/AFP/Getty Images; p. 21 YOSHIKAZU TSUNO/Staff/AFP/Getty Images; p. 22 borchee/E+/Getty Images; p. 24 (top) Koichi Kamoshida/Contributor/Hulton Archive/Getty Images; p. 24 (bottom) Science & Society Picture Library/Contributor/SSPL/Getty Images; p. 25 (top) Mitchell Pettigrew/Moment/Getty Images; p. 25 (bottom) South China Morning Post/Contributor/South China Morning Post/Getty Images; p. 27 VCG/Stringer/Getty Images News/Getty Images; p. 28 (bottom) Star Tribune via Getty Images/Contributor/Star Tribune/Getty Images; p. 29 (top) Imeh Akpanudosen/Contributor/Getty Images Entertainment/Getty Images.

Some of the images in this book illustrate individuals who are models. The depictions do not imply actual situations or events.

CPSIA compliance information: Batch #CS22CSQ: For further information contact Cavendish Square Publishing LLC, New York, New York, at 1-877-980-4450.

Printed in the United States of America

Find us on

CONTENTS

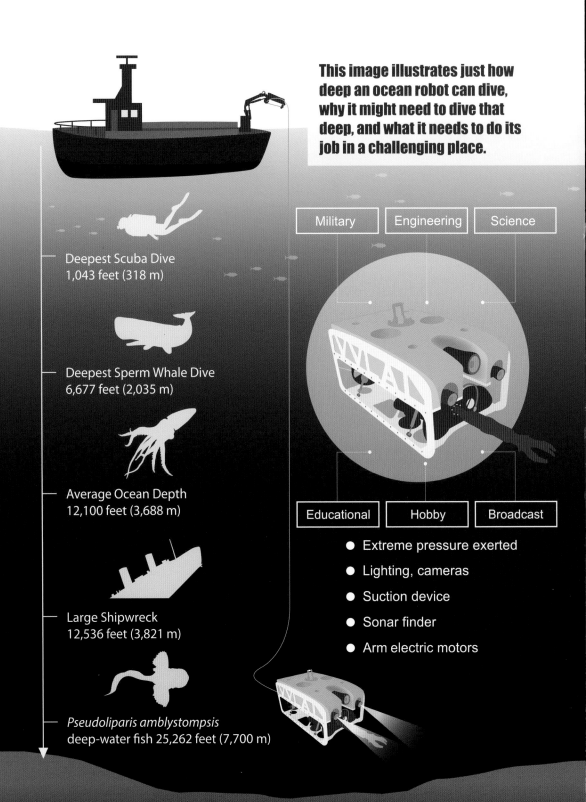

This image illustrates just how deep an ocean robot can dive, why it might need to dive that deep, and what it needs to do its job in a challenging place.

Deepest Scuba Dive
1,043 feet (318 m)

Deepest Sperm Whale Dive
6,677 feet (2,035 m)

Average Ocean Depth
12,100 feet (3,688 m)

Large Shipwreck
12,536 feet (3,821 m)

Pseudoliparis amblystompsis
deep-water fish 25,262 feet (7,700 m)

Military   Engineering   Science

Educational   Hobby   Broadcast

● Extreme pressure exerted
● Lighting, cameras
● Suction device
● Sonar finder
● Arm electric motors

ROBOTS DIVING DEEP

Some robots fly in the air. Some robots go into dangerous places like enemy territory. Some robots are built for the water. Underwater robots can travel to some of the most unreachable places on Earth—even to the deepest trench in the world!

Open Ocean

Scientists know a lot about the ocean, but there's still much to learn. They've identified many marine, or ocean, life-forms. They've explored parts of the ocean floor. Many major underwater discoveries were thanks, in part, to robots.

Scientists have divided the ocean into five layers, or zones. Each zone is darker and colder than the one above it.

Deep-sea divers need to wear special diving suits with hard shells. An atmospheric diving suit (ADS) maintains the surface pressure inside as a person dives deeper into the ocean.

Oceans cover almost three-quarters of our planet, yet nearly 80 percent of these waters haven't yet been mapped or explored. The deep sea is cold and dark, and the pressure of the deep ocean is enough to crush an unprotected person. That makes in-person ocean exploration impossible without the right tools—including robots.

Robots can study ocean currents, explore shipwrecks and ruins, and discover new creatures. Some robots work autonomously, or on their own. Others are controlled by a person remotely, or from a distance. Robots may be the key to exploring the deep sea and uncovering the open ocean's many mysteries.

HOVs, ROVs, and AUVs

Some underwater robots are also called submersibles. Some of the first submersibles were HOVs, or human-occupied vehicles. In 1964, the Woods Hole Oceanographic Institute (WHOI) started using *Alvin*, an HOV that could go 2.8 miles (4.5 kilometers) underwater. It carried two scientists at a time for data collection. This HOV allowed scientists to go into the deep sea without being crushed by the pressure of the ocean.

1. lights
   - allow camera to take footage in ocean darkness

2. camera
   - takes pictures or videos underwater to help a pilot direct the robot

3. frame
   - supports the body of the robot

4. thrusters
   - propel the robot in multiple directions

5. tether
   - allows pilot above water to control the robot remotely
   - sends power and signals between a ship and its ROV

Fast Fact

ROVs are controlled and powered through an umbilical, or tether. This series of cables sends commands from the operator to the ROV.

UUVs are unmanned underwater vehicles. Two kinds of UUVs are remotely operated vehicles (ROVs) and autonomous underwater vehicles (AUVs). ROVs require an operator to direct them from a distance. Operators rely on cameras mounted on the robot to see where it's going in the ocean.

Autonomous underwater vehicles, or AUVs, operate without direct input from an operator. They're preprogrammed with commands. Some AUVs can dive much deeper than ROVs. They can complete their mission on their own.

ROPOS RULES THE SEA!

ROPOS stands for "remotely operated platform for ocean sciences." This ROV is one of the leading underwater robots working today. It is around 10 feet (3 meters) long and 6.5 feet (2 m) tall. It is strong enough to help place a 4,000-pound (1,814 kilogram) piece of scientific equipment on the seafloor. It has high-definition cameras, bright lighting, and arms that can manipulate, or handle, both huge equipment and tiny, breakable coral samples. People direct the movements of ROPOS from a command center on a ship. ROPOS takes footage of the ocean, collects ocean samples, and stores them in bio boxes for testing.

Designing an Underwater Bot

All robots have the same basic parts. They have sensors, which act like the robot's eyes and ears. Sensors gather information about the robot's surroundings, from measuring the temperature to identifying an obstacle in front of it. The controller is like the robot's brain, controlling the robot's actions. Effectors are the parts of the robot that interact with the environment. Actuators are the motors that move the robot's other parts, including its arms or propellers.

Fast Fact

Some AUV controllers use **artificial intelligence** to help them "know" what to do next, while others have a set of actions already programmed. ROVs have remote controls.

Some underwater robots are built in the shape of **torpedoes**, with a thin body and pointed nose. This helps them cut through the water with ease.

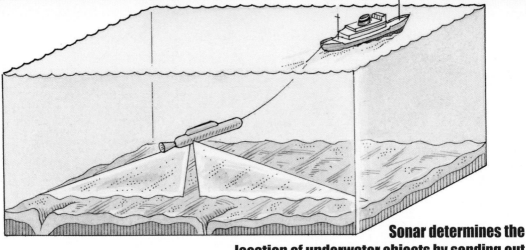

Sonar determines the location of underwater objects by sending out sound waves and measuring how they are reflected back.

Underwater robots are designed for their ocean surroundings. Some have a modular design, which means they have components, or parts, that can be removed and replaced depending on the robot's job. All underwater robots require sensors, navigation equipment, **propulsion** equipment, and a power source.

Some underwater robots have powerful lights so their cameras can work in the deep, dark ocean. Others rely on special sensors that measure magnetic fields, temperatures, or electrical currents. Depth sensors and **sonar** equipment are also necessary. Many underwater robots use propellers to move around. Propellers and other effectors are often powered by rechargeable batteries.

Fast Fact

GPS isn't possible in the deep sea because radio waves can't travel that far. However, an AUV can figure out where it is by using its last known position and how fast and far it's traveled from that point.

Whales use sonar too! This is just one example of how nature can help inform ocean robotics.

Sometimes people live on submarines. Other submarines are autonomous. Some submarines only need to resurface every six months to restock supplies.

Robots perform dangerous jobs so people don't have to risk their lives. They can help locate and recover objects that have been lost in the sea. They can patrol waters and inspect underwater equipment. Let's look at robots at work!

The First Underwater Robots

The late 1800s saw many experiments with underwater technology. Torpedoes became important after their development in 1864. Torpedoes became the first preprogrammed underwater weapons. They were widely used during World War I (1914–1918) and World War II (1939–1945). Pilots dropped torpedoes from planes into water to attack enemy ships and submarines. They were also sent out from submarines or ships.

After World War II, Britain's Royal Navy started using an unmanned submersible called the Cutlet to recover torpedoes and **mines**. In 1957, the University of Washington developed SPURV (special purpose underwater

Fast Fact

An aerial torpedo is a self-propelled missile that is dropped into the water from an airplane or helicopter. The torpedo travels underwater until it reaches its target.

research vehicle). It was the U.S. Navy's first AUV. SPURV collected data through sensors and could dive up to 10,000 feet (3,048 m) deep. In the 1960s, the U.S. Navy developed the cable-controlled underwater recovery vehicle, or CURV, to perform deep-sea rescues and recover objects from the ocean floor. These ROVs and AUVs developed by navies paved the way for the technology used today.

Robot Recon

Robots are masters of reconnaissance. Reconnaissance means surveying an area, especially enemy territory, to learn more information. The military often uses unmanned vehicles for reconnaissance. Unmanned ground vehicles (UGVs), unmanned aerial vehicles (UAVs, or drones), and UUVs

This CURV robot was designed to retrieve objects such as torpedoes from the ocean.

are necessary tools for reconnaissance.

Robots don't require food, oxygen, or rest. They can also be used in dangerous environments. During military operations, sending a robot to complete a mission can save a soldier's life.

Robots can be used to survey enemy waters or guard local ports and harbors. Someday, small UUVs may even inspect each ship that enters a port, making sure there are no dangerous materials aboard. Police departments sometimes use underwater robots to aid in search-and-rescue or recovery operations. This makes robots an important part of law enforcement and military operations at sea.

Recovering the Past

Sometimes robots are the only hope for recovering vehicles, from old ships to downed airplanes, that have been lost to the ocean. The footage and remains that robots can dig up from the deep can help **archaeologists** learn about history and help some families learn more after a disaster like a plane crash.

Underwater vehicles have located and searched many historic shipwrecks, including those of the *Titanic* and the *Bismarck*. These sites could never

Archaeologists are using this UUV to survey ruins of a medieval settlement at the bottom of a lake in Germany.

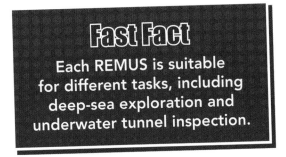

Underwater robots have helped recover items that had been on the *Titanic* when it sank. Robots have played a major role in underwater archaeology.

have been reached by humans alone. The wreckage provides clues about how these ships met their end and who was aboard them.

Some robots are up for seemingly impossible recovery challenges. In 2011, robots found the wreckage of Air France Flight 447 in the southern Atlantic Ocean—two years after it crashed. Underwater robots were able to bring the wreckage and even human remains to the surface.

However, some recovery efforts are too much for even a robot. In 2014, Malaysian Airlines Flight 370 crashed, possibly in the southern Indian Ocean. Officials sent out REMUS (remote environmental monitoring units) robots. Using sonar and other sensors, these robots can gather and record data about the ocean environment. Unfortunately, the search area for the lost Malaysian Airlines flight was very large, and that

Fast Fact

Each REMUS is suitable for different tasks, including deep-sea exploration and underwater tunnel inspection.

UNCOVERING THE TITANIC

The *Titanic* was one of the largest ships of its time. The grand ship was said to be "unsinkable." In April 1912, it set out from Southampton, England, to New York City. However, the ship hit an iceberg in the middle of the Atlantic Ocean and sank, killing around 1,500 people. It wasn't until 1985 that a submersible called *Argo* filmed underwater images of the wreck. Afterward, many submersibles were sent to the wreck to film and take artifacts and pieces of the *Titanic*. The information gained from UUVs helped give scientists and historians a clearer picture about how the mighty ship sunk.

This coffee cup would have been lost forever if underwater robots hadn't had the ability to uncover it from the wreckage of the *Titanic* at the bottom of the Atlantic Ocean.

makes it more challenging for these robots to do their work successfully. Robots have not yet found the resting place of this plane as of early 2021.

In the 1960s, scientists called "aquanauts" lived and worked underwater in Sealab III for days at a time to make underwater discoveries.

Chapter Three

EXPLORE AND LEARN

Underwater robots are a huge help to scientists. Unlike humans, robots can go to the ends of the earth to uncover the incredible **biodiversity** and geography of the oceans. Submersibles take part in scientific studies and deep-sea discoveries, and they can even help forecast some natural disasters.

Scientific Studies

Robots have opened up a whole new world to scientists who want to study the mysteries of the oceans. UUVs have helped scientists discover and identify a wide variety of new plants and animals. Some ocean creatures live in places that are too **extreme** for humans, with intense temperatures and pressures. UUVs have allowed scientists to safely study these plants and animals in their natural environment.

The Monterey Bay Aquarium Research Institute used the Tiburon robot for deep-sea exploration from 1997 to 2008. The Woods Hole Oceanographic Institute also created

Fast Fact

Organisms that live in extreme environments are called "extremophiles." Some bacteria live in **hydrothermal** vents in the Pacific Ocean—a fact that we know today because of robot exploration.

This glider helps scientists study climate change in the Pacific Ocean.

an ROV team—the *Jason* and *Medea* system—for seafloor exploration. The Canadian Scientific Submersible Facility developed the ROPOS robot to explore ocean vents and fix ocean observatories.

Today, UUVs are used to gather data about ocean currents, temperature, and sea life to help people study the effects of climate change. Long-lasting UUVs called gliders patrol the Arctic, collecting data about ocean temperature and the amount of salt and oxygen in the water. Other robots keep an eye on the increased acidity of ocean waters, which can affect the creatures that live there.

Fast Fact

Gliders are AUVs that are powered by their own up-and-down motion. Some take part in six-month missions at sea on their own.

Exploring the Deep

The deep sea is still very much a mystery. Anything we know about the deep sea is dependent on underwater robotic technology. From special diving suits to submersibles, explorers and scientists have developed many tools to safely explore the ocean depths.

This Japanese UUV was built to cruise around the deep sea and explore the seafloor.

Underwater robots can survive the extreme pressure and low temperatures of the deep sea. Their sensors are also capable of detecting things in the darkness that human eyes would never be able to see.

In 2020, it was reported that two ROVs—*Argus* and *Hercules*—had found 30 new species of deep-sea life near the Galapágos Islands. They helped scientists discover new kinds of corals, sea sponges, and crustaceans. These discoveries are important because they help **conservation** efforts in these areas. Someday

Robotic engineers are designing new deep-sea UUVs to explore the deepest parts of the ocean every year.

JOURNEY TO THE CHALLENGER DEEP

The Challenger Deep is the deepest point known on Earth. It's in the Mariana Trench, which is located in the Pacific Ocean. While the average depth of the ocean is 12,100 feet (3,688 m), the Challenger Deep is about 36,200 feet (11,033.8 m) deep. That's about 6 miles (9.7 km) under the water's surface. Very few people have been to the Challenger Deep. In 1960, oceanographer Jacques Piccard and U.S. Navy Lt. Don Walsh made it to the Challenger Deep for the first time—for only about 20 minutes. In 2012, filmmaker James Cameron journeyed to the Challenger Deep with his submersible *Deepsea Challenger*, taking valuable footage and collecting geological and biological samples.

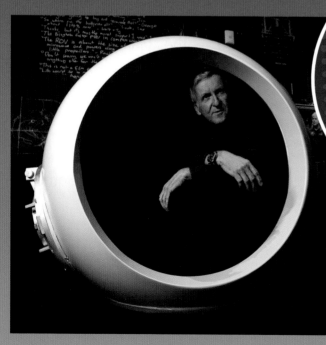

Fast Fact

More than 1,500 circuit boards were built for use aboard the *Deepsea Challenger,* and more than 180 systems operate during dives.

Filmmaker and deep-sea explorer James Cameron made the movie *Titanic* about the historic shipwreck. He also journeyed to the Challenger Deep in an HOV.

soon, artificial intelligence may allow robots not only to collect data but also to identify objects all on their own.

Predicting Disaster

Natural disasters can be deadly, especially if they catch people by surprise. Underwater robots can keep an eye on ocean conditions to help scientists predict a disaster. This can help people prepare for the worst.

The National Oceanic and Atmospheric Association (NOAA) sends UUV gliders out into the Atlantic Ocean to study ocean conditions ahead of hurricane season. The gliders can report the water temperature and the amount of salt, which can give people a clue about how strong hurricanes might be.

In 2017, scientists sent out an AUV called the Wave Glider to waters near a Japanese island called Nishinoshima. The island is an active volcano, and an eruption could trigger a **tsunami** that could hit other islands. The surfboard-like Wave Glider UUV surveys the volcano and can alert people if there's a risk of a tsunami.

This UUV investigates the effect an earthquake had on the seafloor in Japan.

Sea animals such as dolphins swim through the ocean with ease. What might an engineer learn from their body shape and fins?

NEW ROBOTS, NEW OPPORTUNITIES

The ocean presents many challenges to exploration. Engineers continue to build new underwater robot designs for robots that can work smarter, explore farther, and collect more data. What will the underwater robots of tomorrow look like, and how can they help us?

Learning from Nature

Ocean creatures can be great inspiration for robotics engineers. The bodies and behaviors of these animals give engineers ideas for new robots. That's a kind of biomimicry, or a method of solving engineering problems by studying things in nature and **mimicking** them.

Fast Fact

Engineers study birds and insects to design better flying robots, or drones.

Engineers try to copy how sea animals move in water to learn how to build a better underwater robot. Scientists and engineers are designing new underwater robots with flexible body parts that will allow the robots to move through the water the way a fish does. Other designs mimic the gliding motion of manta rays. Lobster bodies inspired an eight-legged robot designed to move along the bottom of smaller bodies of water.

This underwater robot looks and moves like a jellyfish.

New designs may change the face of underwater robots.

Robot, Camera, Action!

Underwater robots can capture amazing footage for entertainment and education, and they can show people underwater wonders. Modern UUVs are cheap, maneuverable, and easy to operate. That makes them useful tools for filming underwater, especially in spaces that are too small for a human diver to reach.

Major documentaries filmed underwater include *Deep Sea* (2006), *Mission Blue* (2014), and

Fast Fact

Engineers are developing soft-bodied robotic fish so the robots can get closer to marine life in their natural **habitats**.

This RoboTuna UUV, introduced around 2000, mimicked a fish.

UUVs can follow ocean animals as they migrate, capturing footage of these animals in action.

Planet Earth: Blue Planet II (2017). The producers of *Blue Planet II* were able to put a camera on a robot to film **bioluminescent** creatures far beneath the water's surface.

UUVs can also record underwater footage of water sports such as swimming, surfing, and fishing. They allow operators to zoom and get multiple angles of these things during fast-paced competition. As UUVs become more advanced, we're likely to see more opportunities for underwater footage in entertainment.

This person is using UUV technology to observe his friends as they take part in underwater sports. The UUV allows him to be up close to the action even though he may not be able to go in the water.

Fast Fact

The 2012 and 2016 Summer Olympics used underwater robotic cameras to capture footage of diving and swimming competitions.

Building the Bots of the Future

Operating robots isn't only for professionals. Just as flying drones has become a popular hobby, operating UUVs can be a fun hobby too. If you're interested in engineering, you can try to build your own UUV. Many homemade underwater robots are built using PVC piping, or the white pipes used in many plumbing systems. You can add lights, cameras, or other sensors to your homemade robot, depending on what you want your robot to do.

Once you've built and tested your underwater robot, you might want to enter it in a competition. The Marine Advanced Technology Education (MATE) Center hosts a popular underwater robotics competition. Schools, colleges, and other organizations compete against each other, building their own robots and using them

Fast Fact

The 2014 documentary *Underwater Dreams* followed the real-life story of teens—sons of Mexican immigrants—who built an underwater robot and won the MATE Center competition.

These underwater robots competed at the World Robot Conference in Beijing, China, in 2016.

ROBOTS SAVE THE OCEANS!

What if robots didn't just study the oceans but left them cleaner as well? A large amount of plastic garbage ends up in the ocean. In fact, there are five massive zones of plastic in the world's oceans, including the Great Pacific Garbage Patch. This zone of swirling plastic is twice the size of Texas! The California-based organization Clear Blue Sea developed a robot that could clean up garbage. It's called the Floating Robot for Eliminating Debris, or FRED. Students contributed ideas to this robot. While FRED isn't ready to take on the Great Pacific Garbage Patch just yet, it shows the promise of how robots can help our oceans.

to perform a series of tasks. These competitions encourage new ideas in the field of marine robotics.

Can you imagine the robots of the future? They might be inspired by sea creatures. They might be small enough to blend into a school of fish. They might spend years at the bottom of the ocean, discovering new creatures and landscapes. Maybe you'll build the new underwater robots of tomorrow!

Young engineers create new UUV technology. Their ideas can shape our understanding of what's underneath the surface of the ocean.

1. What are some situations in which a robot could be used in place of a person under water?

2. Why do you think it's important to find and study the wreckage of ships and planes that have sunk to the bottom of the ocean?

3. Imagine you're sending a UUV to the deepest point of the ocean. What kinds of sensors and abilities would you give the UUV and why?

4. Think of two ways autonomous underwater robots could help combat climate change or natural disasters.

archaeologist: A scientist who studies material remains of past human life and activities.

artificial intelligence: An area of computer science that deals with giving machines the ability to think and act like humans.

biodiversity: The number of different types of living things that are found in a certain place on Earth.

bioluminescent: Having to do with creatures that can produce light through chemical reactions in their bodies.

conservation: Efforts to care for the natural world.

extreme: More than what is expected.

GPS: A navigating system that uses satellite signals to tell the user where they are and direct them to a destination.

habitat: The natural home for plants, animals, and other living things.

hydrothermal: Of or relating to hot water.

mimic: To copy the way something looks, acts, or sounds.

mine: An explosive often buried in the ground or hidden underwater.

propulsion: A force that moves something forward.

sonar: A machine or method that uses sound waves to find things in a body of water.

torpedo: A rocket-shaped exploding device that travels underwater.

tsunami: A large ocean wave that is caused by an earthquake along the floor of the ocean.

Books

Silverman, Buffy. *Surviving a Shipwreck: The Titanic*. Minneapolis, MN: Lerner Publications, 2019.

Spilsbury, Louise, and Richard Spilsbury. *Incredible Robots Underwater*. Oxford, UK: Raintree, 2018.

Troupe, Thomas Kingsley. *Underwater Robots*. Mankato, MN: Black Rabbit Books, 2018.

Websites

Deepsea Challenge
www.deepseachallenge.com
Read more about James Cameron's *Deepsea Challenge*, including facts about the film, expedition, and the submersible that made it all possible.

ROV Jason/Medea
www.whoi.edu/what-we-do/explore/underwater-vehicles/ndsf-jason/
Discover the amazing *Jason* and *Medea* ROV system used by the Woods Hole Oceanographic Institution.

What Is an AUV?
oceanexplorer.noaa.gov/facts/auv.html
Check out facts about AUVs from NOAA.